Martin Luther King Jr.

A LIFE OF DETERMINATION

by Sheila Rivera

Lerner Publications Company • Minneapolis

Photo Acknowledgments

The photographs in this book are reproduced with the courtesy of: © Carol Simowitz, p. 4; © Hulton-Deutsch Collection/CORBIS, p. 6; © Bettmann/CORBIS, pp. 7, 10, 14, 15, 19, 20, 22; Archives Collection, Birmingham Public Library, Birmingham, AL, p. 8; Library of Congress, p. 11; © The Illustrated London News, p. 12; © Washington Post; reprinted by permission of the D.C. Public Library, p. 16; © Flip Schulke/CORBIS, p. 17; National Archives, pp. 18, 24; © Ted Spiegel/CORBIS, p. 25; EyeWire by Getty Images, p. 26.

Front Cover: © Bettmann/CORBIS.

Lerner Publications Company
A division of Lerner Publishing Group
241 First Avenue North
Minneapolis, MN 55401 U.S.A.

Website address: www.lernerbooks.com

Words in **bold type** are explained in a glossary on page 31.

Library of Congress Cataloging-in-Publication Data

Rivera, Sheila, 1970–
    Martin Luther King, Jr.: a life of determination / by Sheila Rivera.
        p.   cm. – (Pull ahead books)
    Includes index.
    ISBN-13: 978-0-8225-3477-8 (lib. bdg. : alk. paper)
    ISBN-10: 0-8225-3477-0 (lib. bdg. : alk. paper)
    1. King, Martin Luther, Jr., 1929–1968–Juvenile literature. 2. African
Americans–Biography–Juvenile literature. 3. Civil rights workers–United
States–Biography–Juvenile literature. 4. Baptists–United
States–Clergy–Biography–Juvenile literature. 5. African Americans–Civil
rights–History–20th century–Juvenile literature. I. Title. II. Series.
E185.97.K5R576 2006
323'.092–dc22   2005009041

Manufactured in the United States of America
1 2 3 4 5 6 – JR – 11 10 09 08 07 06

Table of Contents

People celebrate Martin Luther King Jr. Day.

Martin Luther King Jr. Day

In January, Americans **celebrate** a holiday called Martin Luther King Jr. Day. This holiday was named for a special American. Do you know why we celebrate this day in his honor?

Martin Luther King Jr. had big dreams for the people of the United States.

These men tried to stop Martin from speaking.

Some people tried to stop Martin from making his dreams come true. They did not agree with his ideas. But Martin never gave up. He was **determined.**

Only white people could sit in the front of the bus.

Unfair Treatment

When Martin was growing up, black people did not have the same rights that white people had. Laws said that black people could not sit with white people in restaurants or on buses.

Only black students went to this school.

Black children and white children could not go to the same schools.

Martin saw that African Americans were treated unfairly.

Blacks had to use doors marked "colored."

Mahatma Gandhi (center)

Peaceful Ways

When Martin grew up, he read about a man named Mahatma Gandhi. Gandhi lived in India. He did not believe in fighting. He taught people how to **protest** unfair treatment in peaceful ways.

Martin wanted to help black people.

Martin liked Gandhi's ideas. Martin was determined to help black people in the United States.

He showed people how they could work to get fair treatment without fighting.

These people wanted schools to let in both blacks and whites.

Martin gave speeches about the unfair way that blacks were treated. He talked about peace.

He said that everyone should be
treated the same. A person's **race**
or skin color should not matter.

People marched for equal rights.

Martin led people on peaceful
marches. They demanded fair
treatment for everyone.

Some white people did not want blacks to have the same rights as whites. They attacked the marchers.

Some white people yelled at the marchers.

Police officers take Martin to jail.

Determined to Help

Some people got mad at Martin.
The police **arrested** him many times.
But they didn't stop him. Martin was
determined to make change peacefully.

Martin gives his "I have a dream" speech.

Martin's Dream

Martin gave a famous speech in Washington, D.C., on August 28, 1963. He said, "I have a dream that one day little black boys and black girls will be able to join hands with little white boys and white girls as sisters and brothers."

Martin won the **Nobel Peace Prize.**

The prize is a great honor. It is given to someone who works toward peace.

Martin received a Nobel Prize Medal like this one.

Now all people can work and play together.

Changing the World

Martin's determination helped change unfair laws. He taught people that they could change the world in peaceful ways. That is why we celebrate Martin Luther King Jr. Day.

MARTIN LUTHER KING JR. TIMELINE

1929
Martin Luther King Jr. is born in Atlanta, Georgia, on January 15.

1954
The Supreme Court decides that black students and white students can no longer be forced to go to separate schools.

1953
Martin marries Coretta Scott on June 18.

1955
Martin and others in Montgomery, Alabama, protest the unfair way that blacks are treated. They refuse to ride city buses for one day.

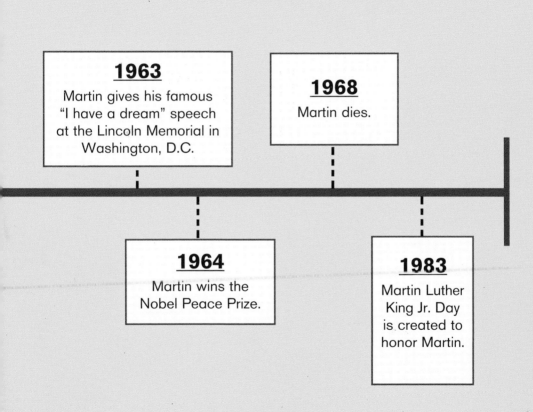

1963
Martin gives his famous "I have a dream" speech at the Lincoln Memorial in Washington, D.C.

1968
Martin dies.

1964
Martin wins the Nobel Peace Prize.

1983
Martin Luther King Jr. Day is created to honor Martin.

More about Martin Luther King Jr.

● Martin studied hard and began college when he was only fifteen years old.

● When Martin won the Nobel Peace Prize, he received $54,000. He gave some of the money to groups who supported equal rights.

● Martin Luther King Jr. Day is celebrated on the third Monday of January every year. This day was chosen because it is close to Martin's birthday.

Websites

The King Center
http://www.thekingcenter.org

Martin Luther King, Jr.
http://www.nps.gov/malu/

Martin Luther King Jr. Day on the Net—The Holiday
http://www.holidays.net/mlk/holiday.htm

Glossary

arrested: taken to jail by the police

celebrate: to have a party or do another activity to honor a special occasion

determined: to be firm in sticking to a purpose

marches: groups of people walking together for a purpose

Nobel Peace Prize: an honor given for a person's work toward peace

protest: to express strong disagreement

race: physical traits shared by a group of people that are passed on from one generation to the next

Index